LIGHTNING BOLT BOOKS™

Experiment with Pollination

Nadia Higgins

Lerner Publications
Minneapolis

Copyright © 2015 by Lerner Publishing Group, Inc.

Content Consultant: Dr. Norm Lownds, Curator, Michigan 4-H Children's Gardens

Lerner Publications Company
A division of Lerner Publishing Group, Inc.
241 First Avenue North
Minneapolis, MN 55401 USA

For reading levels and more information, look up this title at www.lernerbooks.com.

Library of Congress Cataloging-in-Publication Data
Higgins, Nadia.
      Experiment with pollination / by Nadia Higgins.
         pages cm. — (Lightning bolt books ™ — Plant experiments)
      Includes index.
      ISBN 978-1-4677-5734-8 (lib. bdg. : alk. paper)
      ISBN 978-1-4677-6076-8 (pbk.)
      ISBN 978-1-4677-6246-5 (EB pdf)
      1. Pollination—Juvenile literature. 2. Plants—Experiments—Juvenile literature. I. Title.
   II. Series: Lightning bolt books. Plant experiments.
   QK926.H575 2015
   571.8'642—dc23   2014027541

Manufactured in the United States of America
1 — BP — 12/31/14

Table of Contents

What Are the Parts of a Flower?

Colorful flowers fill vases and brighten gardens. Out in nature, beautiful flowers have an important job.

Flower gardens are full of flowers waiting to be pollinated.

Flowers make seeds. Pollination is the first step in making seeds.

Bees aid in pollination.

During pollination, tiny pollen grains move from one flower part to another. Most often, insects carry the pollen from flower to flower.

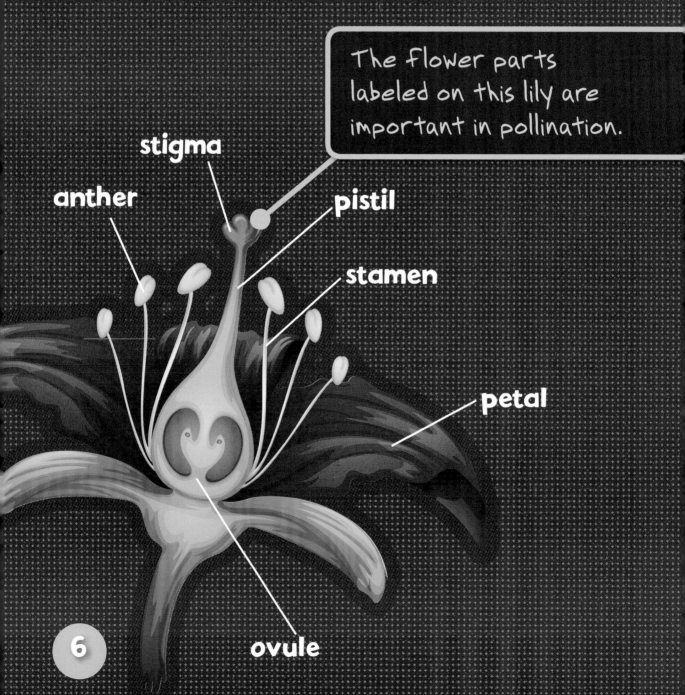

The flower parts labeled on this lily are important in pollination.

stigma

anther

pistil

stamen

petal

ovule

Let's look at the parts of a flower and how they work together during pollination.

What You Need:

tape

pencil and paper

lily

cotton swab

scissors

Steps:

1. Gently pull the petals off the lily. Tape them to the paper, and label them "petals."

2. Pull the stamens off the lily. Tape them to the paper, and label them "stamens." If you aren't sure where a certain part is on your flower, look to the labels on page 6 to help you.

If you're allergic to pollen, have an adult cut off your flower's stamens. For steps 2 and 3, draw the stamens, using the diagram on page 6.

3. Touch the tip of one of the stamens with the cotton swab. Label the tip "anther."

4. Find the pistil and tape it to the paper. Touch its tip. Is it sticky?

5. Use the scissors to slice open the base of the pistil. Cut the long way. Can you see the ovules?

Label the tip of the pistil "stigma."

Think It Through

If the stigma on your lily was sticky, the lily was ready for pollination. It would have used pollen from a different flower to make a seed.

A seed will form only if pollen from the same types of flowers join.

How Do Bees' Bristles Help Flowers?

Pollinators are insects or other animals that spread pollen. As they sip nectar, their bodies pick up pollen. The pollen rubs off on the next flower they visit.

Honeybees use the pollen they pick up to feed their young.

Bees are one of nature's best pollinators. Pollen sticks all over their hairy bodies.

A bumblebee can visit up to forty flowers in one minute!

How much do those tiny hairs help? Let's try this experiment to see!

What You Need:

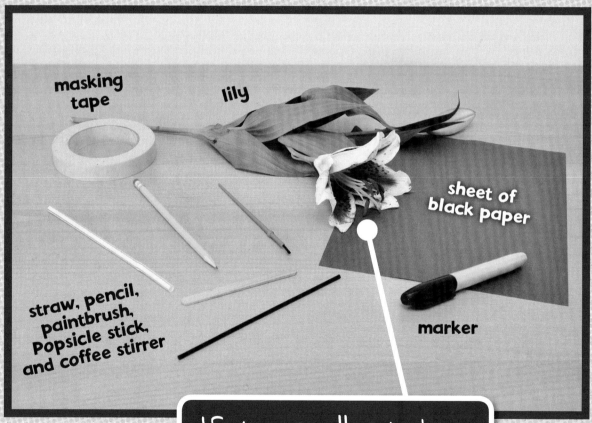

masking tape

lily

sheet of black paper

marker

straw, pencil, paintbrush, Popsicle stick, and coffee stirrer

If you are allergic to pollen, substitute the lily for a bowl filled with baking powder.

Steps:

1. Open up the lily and spread out the stamens.

2. Touch the paintbrush to the first stamen. Then tap the brush on the paper.

Label the mark left by the paintbrush as shown here.

Paintbrush

3. Touch the next stamen with the pencil. Tap the paper, and label the pollen mark "pencil."

4. Repeat step 3 until you've tested the straw, the Popsicle stick, and the coffee stirrer. Do not use the same stamen twice.

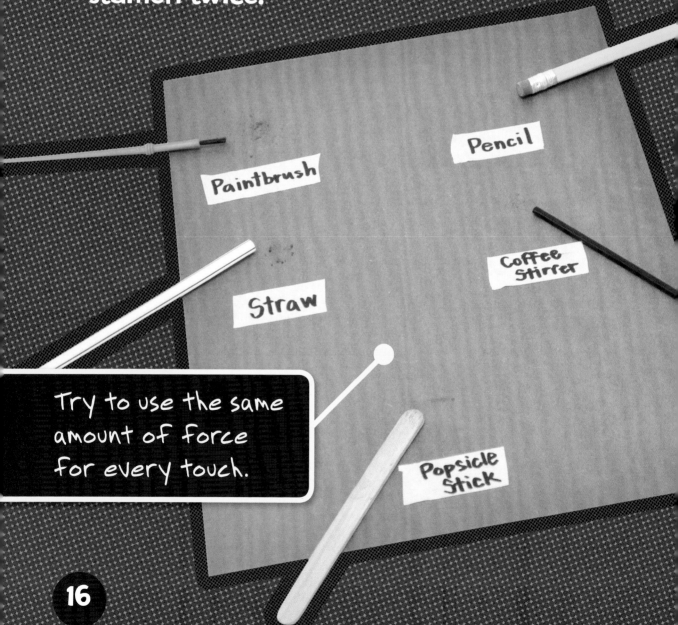

Paintbrush

Pencil

Straw

Coffee Stirrer

Popsicle Stick

Try to use the same amount of force for every touch.

As this butterfly sips nectar, its head gets dusted with pollen.

Think It Through

Did the paintbrush leave the biggest spot? If so, there's a good reason for that! Most pollinators have bristles, fur, or feathers that pollen can stick to. Even a butterfly's head is hairy.

How Do Flowers and Pollinators Work Together?

Some bees have short tongues. These bees visit shallow, open flowers. The bees can easily reach the nectar at the bottom.

The nectar in this flower is easy for bees to get to.

Other flowers are deeper. It may take a long-tongued butterfly or a bird with a long beak to reach the pollen in these flowers. This chart shows which pollinators prefer which types of flowers.

Pollinator	Color	Shape	Smell	Example
Bee	Blue, yellow, white	Not too deep	Sweet, mild	Buttercup
Butterfly	Bright red, yellow, orange, purple	Often narrow tubes or a lot of petals; often in clusters	Faint	Butterfly weed
Bird	Red, yellow, orange	Wide cups or tubes; curved petals; often dangling down	None	Columbine

Can you predict which type of pollinator spreads the pollen of different kinds of flowers?

Let's give *it* a try.

What You Need:

pencil and notebook

four different kinds of flowers

Lilies, dandelions, zinnias, daisies, and marigolds are some flowers that work well for this experiment.

Steps:

1. Observe your flowers and take notes. Notice their color, shape, and smell.

2. Using the chart on page 19, predict how your flowers spread pollen. Is it by bee, butterfly, or bird?

Marigold
- orange
- many petals in a cluster
- faint smell
- pollinator: butterfly

3. Show your predictions to a friend. Explain why you made your choices.

Work with your friends to make predictions about the flowers.

In fall, ragweed fills the air with pollen. It causes allergies for many people.

Think It Through

About nine out of ten flowering plants rely on animals to spread their pollen. Bees and butterflies are common pollinators. Birds are less common pollinators. Still other growing things rely on wind to spread their pollen.

23

What's Inside a Seed?

Once pollen joins an ovule, a flower's job is done. Now the seed can develop inside the fruit that grows around it. What is a seed, exactly? Let's take a closer look.

What You Need:

bowl

water

lima bean seeds

Steps:

1. Add water to the bowl.

2. Add a few lima bean seeds and let them soak overnight.

3. Remove one bean seed. Rub the bean seed with your fingers until the seed coat slips off. If the seed breaks when you remove the seed coat, you can use one of the other seeds in the bowl as a backup.

4. Use your fingers to pull the bean seed into two halves.

5. Can you find the seedling, or baby plant, inside the seed?

What do you think is the purpose of the rest of the seed?

Think It Through

A seed has three main parts. The seed coat protects the seed. This is what you pulled off. The seedling will grow roots and leaves. The rest of the seed is food for the growing plant.

If planted, the seed would eventually begin to sprout.

Dissect Like a Scientist

Scientists dissect plants. This means they take plants apart. This helps scientists see how a plant's parts fit together. Here are some ways to dissect like a scientist:

1. Prepare and clean your work area.

2. Work outward in. First, pull off a flower's petals. Then remove the stamens.

3. Label the flower parts as you find them.

4. Ask lots of questions. Why is this part a particular color or shape?

Fun Facts

- Every flower has its own kind of pollen. You can see the differences using a microscope.

- Lizards and bats are pollinators.

- Each silky thread on an ear of corn is a stigma. There's one thread for every kernel.

- There are more than two hundred thousand animal pollinators.

- Pollinators are responsible for one out of every three bites of food you eat.

Glossary

anther: the tip of the stamen that is coated with pollen

nectar: the sweet liquid that flowers make to attract pollinators

ovule: the part of the flower that grows into a seed once it joins with pollen

pistil: the part of a flower that receives pollen

pollen: a powdery substance that joins with eggs to make seeds

pollination: spreading pollen from one flower to another

pollinator: something that spreads pollen from one flower to another

stamen: a part of a flower that holds pollen

stigma: the tip of the pistil that sticks to pollen

Further Reading

Brooklyn Botanic Garden:
Young Readers Articles
http://www.bbg.org/gardening
/category/young_readers

Hirsch, Rebecca E. *Science Lab: The Life Cycles of Plants.* Ann Arbor, MI: Cherry Lake, 2011.

Kids Growing Strong: Pollinator Garden
http://kidsgrowingstrong.org/PollinatorGarden

Markle, Sandra. *The Case of the Vanishing Honeybees: A Scientific Mystery.* Minneapolis: Lerner Publications, 2014.

PollinatorLIVE
http://pollinatorlive.pwnet.org

VanCleave, Janice Pratt. *Step-by-Step Science Experiments in Biology.* New York: Rosen, 2013.

Index

Photo Acknowledgments

The images in this book are used with the permission of: © Rick Orndorf, pp. 2, 7, 9, 10, 14, 15, 16, 20, 21, 24, 25, 26; © Artens/Shutterstock Images, p. 4; © szefei/Shutterstock Images, p. 5; © BlueRingMedia/Shutterstock Images, p. 6; © Dean Fikar/Shutterstock Images, p. 8; © Thinkstock, pp. 11, 18; © Klagyivik Viktor/Shutterstock Images, p. 12; © Sailorr/Shutterstock Images, p. 13; © Tagstock1/Shutterstock Images, p. 17; © motorolka/Shutterstock Images, p. 19 (top); © Mark Herreid/Shutterstock Images, p. 19 (center); © Ijh images/Shutterstock Images, p. 19 (bottom); © wavebreakmedia/Shutterstock Images, p. 22; © Melinda Fawver/Shutterstock Images, p. 23; © Marie C Fields/Shutterstock Images, p. 27; © Susan Law Cain/Shutterstock Images, p. 28; © Es75/Shutterstock Images, p. 30; © Birdiegal/Shutterstock Images, p. 31.

Front cover: © iStockphoto.com/Tsekhmister.

Main body text set in Johann Light 30/36.